DEVELOPING MATHEMATICS

**Customisable
teaching resources
for mathematics**

UNDERSTANDING SHAPES AND MEASURES

Ages 4-5

**Hilary Koll and
Steve Mills**

A & C Black • London

Contents

Understanding shape

Use familiar objects and common shapes to create and recreate patterns and build models

Use language such as 'circle' and 'bigger' to describe the shape and size of solids and flat shapes

Use everyday words to describe position

Measuring

Use language such as 'greater', 'smaller', 'heavier' or 'lighter' to compare quantities

Use everyday language related to time; order and sequence familiar events and measure short periods of time

---

Published 2008 by A & C Black Publishers Limited
36 Soho Square, London W1D 3QY
www.acblack.com

ISBN 978-1-4081-0060-8

Copyright text © Hilary Koll and Steve Mills 2008
Copyright illustrations © Gaynor Berry 2008
Copyright cover illustration © Jan McCafferty 2008
Editors: Lynne Williamson and Marie Lister
Designed by Billin Design Solutions Ltd

The authors and publishers would like to thank Catherine Yemm and Judith Wells for their advice in producing this series of books.

A CIP catalogue record for this book is available from the British Library.

Printed and bound in Great Britain by Halstan Printing Group, Amersham, Buckinghamshire.

A & C Black uses paper produced with elemental chlorine-free pulp, harvested from managed sustainable forests.

Introduction

The 100% New Developing Mathematics Understanding Shapes and Measures is a series of seven photocopiable activity books for children aged 4 to 11 designed to be used during the daily maths lesson. The books focus on the skills and concepts for Understanding Shapes and Measuring as outlined in the National Strategy's *Primary Framework for literacy and mathematics*. The activities are intended to be used in the time allocated to pupil activities; they aim to reinforce the knowledge and develop the facts, skills and understanding explored during the main part of the lesson and to provide practice and consolidation of the objectives contained in the Framework document.

Understanding shape

The 'Understanding Shape' strand of the *Primary Framework for mathematics* is concerned with helping pupils to develop awareness and understanding of the properties of shapes, special concepts and ideas of position and location. This strand includes the properties of 2-D and 3-D shapes, including angles and symmetries together with ways of describing positions in grids such as using co-ordinates.

Measuring

The 'Measuring' strand of the *Primary Framework for mathematics* covers the main measurement topics such as length, mass and capacity, together with ideas of time, area and perimeter. These topics include estimating, comparing and measuring including using standard metric units and converting between them.

Understanding Shapes and Measures Ages 4–5

supports the teaching of mathematics by providing a series of activities to develop spatial vocabulary in order to increase awareness of properties of shape and measurement concepts. On the whole, the activities are designed for children to work on independently, although due to the young age of the children, the teacher may need to read the instructions with the children to ensure that they understand the activity before they begin working on it.

The following objectives are covered:

- use familiar objects and common shapes to create and recreate patterns and build models;
- use language such as 'circle' and 'bigger' to describe the shape and size of solids and flat shapes;
- use everyday words to describe position;
- use language such as 'greater', 'smaller', 'heavier' or 'lighter' to compare quantities;

- use everyday language related to time; order and sequence familiar events and measure short periods of time.

Extension

Many of the activity sheets end with a challenge (**Now try this!**) which reinforces and extends the children's learning, and provides the teacher with an opportunity for assessment. Again, it may be necessary to read the instructions with the children before they begin the activity. For some challenges the children may require additional paper.

Organisation

Very little equipment is needed, but it will be useful to have the following resources available: coloured pencils, sticky shapes, scissors, glue, pastry cutters, dice, counters, 2-D shapes, solid shapes, balance scales, cubes, one-minute sand timer.

Where possible, the children's work should be supported by ICT equipment. It is also vital that children's experiences are introduced in real-life contexts and through practical activities. The teachers' notes at the foot of each page and the more detailed notes on pages 6 to 13 suggest ways in which this can be done effectively.

To help teachers select appropriate learning experiences for the children, the activities are grouped into sections within the book. However, the activities are not expected to be used in this order unless stated otherwise. The sheets are intended to support, rather than direct, the teacher's planning.

Accompanying CD

The enclosed CD-ROM contains all of the activity sheets from the book and a program that allows you to edit them for printing or saving. This means that modifications can be made to further differentiate the activities to suit individual pupils' needs. See page 14 for further details.

Teachers' notes

Brief notes are provided at the foot of each page, giving ideas and suggestions for maximising the effectiveness of the activity sheets. These can be masked before copying. Further explanations of the activities can be found on pages 6 to 13, together with examples of questions that you can ask.

Whole class warm-up activities

The tools provided in A & C Black's Maths Skills and Practice CD-ROMs can be used as introductory activities for use with the whole class. In the Maths Skills and Practice CD-ROM R (ISBN 9780713673166) the following activities and games could be used to introduce or reinforce 'Shapes and Measures' objectives:

- Area quiz
- Measurement
- The maze
- Position
- 2-D shape sort
- 3-D shape sort
- Weight quiz
- Shape pictures

The following activities provide some practical ideas that can be used to introduce or reinforce the main teaching part of the lesson, or provide an interesting basis for discussion.

Mystery shapes

Place a selection of 2-D (or 3-D) shapes into a feely bag. Put your hand inside and either describe one of the shapes and what it feels like or encourage the children to ask you questions about what you can feel, for example, *Does it have straight or curved sides? How many corners has it?* Children can be asked to either say the name of the shape that they think it might be or to choose the shape from another set of shapes. The shape should then be withdrawn and compared with the children's answers.

Which wall?

Ideally, this game should be played in a hall or large room. Around the walls place several pictures of 2-D shapes, for example a triangle, a square, a rectangle, a circle and a hexagon. Ask the children to stand in the centre of the room. Begin to describe one of the shapes and ask the children to stand next to the picture of the shape that they think it is, for example *This shape has only straight sides. All the sides are the same length. The shape has 4 corners.* The same activity can be played where large 3-D shapes are positioned around the room such as a cone, a cube, a pyramid, etc.

Word wizard

Encourage the children to develop and use a range of vocabulary by playing 'Word wizard'. Call out a measurement word and ask the children to say the word that means the opposite, for example 'taller/shorter', 'heavier/lighter', 'wider/narrower', 'thicker/thinner', 'longer/shorter', etc. As the children give a word correctly, hold up two objects to compare and ask them to correctly say sentences using each of the words, for example *The blue pencil is longer than the red pencil. The red pencil is shorter than the blue pencil.*

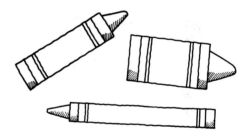

Time warnings

During everyday classroom activities encourage the children to estimate lengths of time by giving time warnings such as: *In five minutes time Mrs Jones will take her group. Playtime will be in 10 minutes. In one minute I want you to line up.* etc. Point out the time on the clock at the beginning of the time warning and then again at the time of the event. As children develop an improved awareness, individuals can be set time warnings of their own, for example *In two minutes I want you to go and sit on the carpet. In five minutes, James is going to tell us about his holiday.* Make sure that time warnings are followed through to ensure that the children develop an appropriate sense of time passing.

Notes on the activities

Understanding shapes

Use familiar objects and common shapes to create and recreate patterns and build models

It is vital that young children are given extensive opportunity to work practically with shapes, construction materials, boxes, containers, sand, water and so on, both in play and in more structured activities. The following activities can supplement these practical tasks and provide contexts and stimuli that can be more fully explored in the classroom. Stories and rhymes can also be used as starting points for activities. Encourage children to develop vocabulary skills by ensuring that these activities are undertaken in pairs or small groups and that whole class discussions take place frequently.

Make the animals (page 15)

Sticky shapes are a wonderful classroom resource, which invite children to make pictures and patterns whilst exploring and becoming familiar with the properties and names of the shapes. Encourage children to describe the shapes used to make the animals using words such as straight and curved together with any shape names that are known. With this extension activity, and the one on the following page, it is not essential that children directly copy the animals or cars but see the potential for things that can be made with shapes. When discussing the shapes that have been used to make the pictures on the sheet, ensure that the children are able to name the shapes that are only partially shown. Also, provide scissors so that the children can, for example, cut a square in half to make a rectangle. Discuss the names of shapes that they make in this way.

SUGGESTED QUESTIONS:

• What shape have you used here?
• How many triangles can you see?

• Is this shape round?
• How many circles have you used to make this animal?

Make the cars (page 16)

See the notes for the previous page.

SUGGESTED QUESTIONS:

• What shape are the wheels?
• How many rectangles have been used to make this car?
• Which shapes have you used to make your car?
• Are the sides of your car curved or straight?

Stripy scarves (page 17)

Repeating colour patterns are a useful way of exploring repetition and are a precursor to repeating patterns involving shapes. Children notice repeating colour patterns before they are able to recognise repeating shape patterns as the ability to distinguish between different shapes is more complex. At the start of the lesson, examine different ways of using colours to make repeating patterns to ensure that the children know what is expected of them. Be alert for children who display any signs of colour blindness, particularly with red/green colours. The children could bring in stripy scarves from home to include as part of a class display of patterns.

SUGGESTED QUESTIONS:

• Which colour comes next?
• What pattern have you chosen to make?

Shape bracelets (page 18)

Shape bracelets are a fun, colourful way of exploring repeating shape patterns and, if taped correctly, show how a repeating pattern can go on and on forever. Display colour words for the children to see to help them match the colour words with the correct colours.

As a follow-on activity children could make bracelets for a giant, using larger paper and perhaps potato printing repeating patterns. These could then form hanging displays in the classroom.

SUGGESTED QUESTIONS:

• Choose one of your bracelets and tell me the pattern it shows.
• What do you call this shape?
• Do you know another word for 'round'?
• How many corners does this shape have?

Guess the cake! (page 19)

The focus of this activity is on recognising and continuing repeating patterns in order to find which cake the child at the end of the row will get. It encourages predicting and visualising skills. The children can draw their own repeating patterns in the same way.

SUGGESTED QUESTIONS:

• Which cake do you think each child might get?
• Why do you think it will be that cake?
• Can you draw a cake repeating pattern of your own?

The great shape game (page 20)

These shape cards are best copied onto thick paper or card and laminated for a more permanent resource. Encourage the children to match up the pieces in different ways to make shapes. You will find that children like to match up the sides of the shapes carefully and so will produce complete circles, squares, rectangles and triangles. Invite them to make as many different shapes as they can with the pieces and to make a record of them by drawing them on paper.

In the plenary, ask the children to show the drawings of the shapes that they made and to summarise what they have made, for example 'We made three circles and two squares'. These drawings/markings can provide a fascinating insight into children's perceptions of shapes and their properties.)

SUGGESTED QUESTIONS:

* What shape have you made here?
* Can you draw it for me?
* How many sides/corners does it have?
* Are its sides curved or straight?

Pastry cutting (page 21)

This activity should follow on from practical work of cutting shapes from rolled out modelling clay.

To make your own clay (salt dough):

Mix and knead ingredients in the following proportions:

1 part salt (to make them inedible)

2 parts flour

1 part water

The clay can be rolled out using a rolling pin and shape cutters used to make shapes.

If desired, shapes can be baked at 140°C for about 1 hour or until golden and hard. Cool and paint. Shapes can be preserved further by painting with clear varnish.

SUGGESTED QUESTIONS:

* What is the name of this shape?
* How many triangles can you see?
* Are its sides curved or straight?
* Are these two shapes the same?
* What is different about them?
* How many corners do they have they?

Gift bags (page 22)

This activity can form part of a wider topic on presents, festivals or celebrations. Encourage the children to bring in any gift bags they may have and build up a collection of them. Encourage comparison of the bags using words such as tallest, widest, largest, smallest, shortest, thinnest, narrowest etc. and examine the shapes decorating the bags.

SUGGESTED QUESTIONS:

* What shape have you drawn here?
* How many sides/corners/edges does it have?
* Are its sides curved or straight?
* How many have you drawn?
* Which is the largest shape you have drawn?

Making models (page 23)

Children should work in pairs or small groups for this activity. They will need a range of solid shapes and a dice. Ensure they understand how a 'key' works and how the dice indicates

which solid shape they should select. If the children make their own models, they could sketch them on the back of the sheet.

SUGGESTED QUESTIONS:

* What shape is this?
* What is special about it?
* Has it got corners?
* Are its faces curved or flat?
* Which is the larger of these two shapes?
* What is different about these two shapes?

Use language such as 'circle' and 'bigger' 'to describe the shape and size of solids and flat shapes

All of the activities above and those below can be used to encourage the children to develop language skills and to develop awareness of the properties of shapes. Words that children should begin to develop an understanding of, and begin to use themselves in everyday language, include:

shape, flat, curved, straight, round, hollow, solid, corner, sharp, pointed, smooth, jagged, zigzag, face, side, wiggly, loopy, wavy, edge, end, sort, make, build, model, cube, pyramid, sphere, cone, circle, triangle, square, rectangle, size, bigger, larger, smaller, middle-sized, pattern, repeating pattern, match, line, different, same...

Shape matching: 1 and 2 (pages 24 and 25)

For this activity the children will need to be given scissors. Should this prove to be too difficult for any of the children several sets of the shapes could already be pre-cut and stored in envelopes to distribute as appropriate. Ideally these sets would be laminated to be used in play areas and as a more permanent resource. Children could bring in shells and group them according to their particular shapes, or whether they are smooth or jagged.

SUGGESTED QUESTIONS:

* Which shell looks sharpest?
* Which one is round?
* Do you know the name of this shape?
* How many pointy corners has this shape?
* Are the sides of this shell smooth/jagged?

Doing lines (page 26)

Tracing over dotted lines can help children to observe the different properties of the lines and to describe them using appropriate words.

SUGGESTED QUESTIONS:

- What is special about this line?
- How is it different from this line?
- Which line is straight?

Super-shape heroes: 1–4 (pages 27, 28, 29 and 30)

The super-shape heroes can be an on-going story or context that children become familiar with over time. Stories can be told about the super-shape heroes: triangle-man, circle-woman, rectangle-man and square-woman. The more interesting and varied the stories of their antics are, the more children will picture them and remember the attributes of the shapes they are made from. They can form interesting classroom displays, be enlarged, copied and then coloured/painted in different colours. These sheets can be given to children individually to give them an opportunity to study the shapes and draw further ones of their own.

SUGGESTED QUESTIONS:

- What shape is this super-hero?
- What is special about him/her?
- Look at the shapes he/she is made from.
- Have the shapes got corners? How many?
- Are the sides of the shapes curved or straight?
- Which is the largest of the shapes in his/her body?

3-D shapes (page 31)

It is important that the children have as much experience with

actual solid shapes as possible. Similar items such as those shown could be placed in a set and the children asked to find any that are the same shape and sort them into groups. Encourage discussion and comparison of the shapes, drawing attention to features such as bigger, smaller, curved, straight etc. Be aware that some children find associating 2-D pictures of 3-D shapes with the solid shapes themselves quite difficult. To assess this, you could ask the children to choose objects to match those on the sheets.

SUGGESTED QUESTIONS:

- Which two shapes are the same?
- What is special about them?
- Which is the larger of the two shapes?
- What is different about these two shapes?

2-D shapes (page 32)

The extension activity for this task involves finding the odd one out in a set. The final one shows three squares and a rectangle. Many children find this difficult as all the shapes have four corners. If a child does not correctly identify the non-square rectangle it is likely to be because he/she has not appreciated that squares have equal sides. Invite the child to say why he/she ticked that particular shape. Reasons may include orientation as many children fail to appreciate that a certain shape, for example a square, remains a square whatever its orientation.

SUGGESTED QUESTIONS:

- Which two shapes are the same?
- What is special about them?
- Which is the larger of the two shapes?
- What is different about these two shapes?

Use everyday words to describe position

Words that children should begin to develop an understanding of, and begin to use themselves in everyday language, include:

position, over, under, above, below, beneath,
top, bottom, side, on, in, outside, inside, around,
in front, behind, front, back, before, after,
beside, next to, opposite, apart, between,
middle, edge, corner, direction, left, right,
up, down, forwards, backwards, sideways,
across, close, far, near, along, through, to,
from, towards, away from, movement,
slide, roll, turn, stretch, bend

Move the cube (page 33)

These cards can be used in a variety of ways for whole class, individual, or group activities.

The cards can be cut out and used as follows:

1. As a whole class activity each child can be given a cube. A card is selected at random, such as from a bag, and a child chosen to move the cube according to the instruction, for example, move the cube so that it is 'near your foot', or 'in a corner of the room'. Sometimes this will involve the child moving around the classroom, others will involve just moving the cube without changing location.

2. The cut-out cards can be used as forfeits in a game of Pass-the-parcel. Rather than moving the cube, the wrapping paper that has come off can be moved to the position shown before then being placed in the bin.

3. Children can work in pairs or small groups and take it in turns to pick a card and move the cube to that location.

4. The cards could be laminated and kept in a bag in the classroom. In spare moments, for example when children are waiting in line, a child could be selected to pick a card and take a cube to the location shown.

5. The children could pick a card from the bag and not show anyone then move the cube and his/her classmates have to guess what might have been written on the card.

SUGGESTED QUESTIONS:

• Where have you put the cube?
• Is there another way of saying that?
• Does 'close to' mean the same as 'near to'?
• I'm holding the cube here. How could you describe where the cube is?

Put Peter in the picture (page 34)

This activity can follow on nicely from the previous activity. Children, working in pairs, should cut out Peter and move him around the picture into different positions. Encourage the children to tell a story as they do this about Peter's day and to use a range of vocabulary to describe where he is. Peter can eventually be stuck down in one location and the class's pictures of him in different positions displayed on the wall with the associated words, for example: Peter is **in** the tent, Peter is **on** the swing, Peter is **near** the river, Peter is **under** the tree, Peter is **next** to the dog, Peter is **far from** the car etc. As a class activity, move Peter to different locations and ask questions about his location. This activity would also work well if the sheet were enlarged to A3 then laminated and used with a small group. Each child could take it in turns to tell the story of Peter's day. The children in this case could be encouraged to make each story different, for example in one story Peter could fly high on the swing, in another he could fall off it and hurt himself!

SUGGESTED QUESTIONS:

• Where have you put Peter?
• Tell me where he is now.
• Is he far from or close to the car?
• Is he under or over the tree?

Where's Claire? (page 35)

Encourage the children to talk to each other in pairs so that they begin to realise that there are many different ways of describing the same location, for example beside a lamp, near to a lamp, close to a lamp, next to a lamp, etc. As a further extension activity the children can draw Claire in other locations such as on a table, under a table, beside a table **or** in a car, beside a car, far from a car, etc.

SUGGESTED QUESTIONS:

• Where is Claire?
• Tell me where she is in this picture.
• Can you draw her in (say location)?

Mousey, mousey... (page 36)

Children may need help with reading the text. The pictures on this page could be enlarged and used for classroom displays, encouraging the children to match the correct position word with the correct picture.

SUGGESTED QUESTIONS:

• Where is the mouse?
• Is the mouse in the cup or on the cup?
• Can you draw the mouse in (say location)?

Draw a ladybird (page 37)

This activity is best done with a small stuffed toy (ideally a ladybird) or a large cut-out ladybird with putty on. Throughout each day, reposition the ladybird around the classroom and ask the children to find it and say where it is. Ask questions about its location, offering suggestions to model the words correctly, for example 'Is it opposite the door?' 'Is it close to or far from the bin?' etc.

SUGGESTED QUESTIONS:

• Where is the ladybird?
• Is there another way you could say where it is?
• How would you say where it was?

The 'What is?' game (page 38)

For cross-curricular work, this activity could be linked to the story of *Goldilocks and the Three Bears*.

SUGGESTED QUESTIONS:

• What is above the chair?
• What is below the bed?
• What is next to the spoon?

Measuring

Use language such as 'greater', 'smaller, 'heavier' or 'lighter' to compare quantities

Words that children should begin to develop an understanding of, and begin to use themselves in everyday language, include:

measure, size, compare, guess, estimate,
enough, not enough, too much, too little,
nearly, close to, about the same as, just over, just under,
length, width, height, depth, long, short, tall,
high, low, wide, narrow, deep, shallow, thick, thin,
longer, shorter, taller, higher... and so on,
longest, shortest, tallest, highest... and so on,
far, near, close, weigh, weighs, balances,
heavy/light, heavier/lighter, heaviest/lightest,
balance, weight, scales, full, half-full, empty,
holds, container

I spy... (page 39)

For this activity the children will need a counter each and one dice for the group. If possible, an adult could work with the children to help with the reading and for checking answers. The sheet could be enlarged to A3 to make it easier for children to work with.

SUGGESTED QUESTIONS:

- What can you see that is taller than an umbrella?
- Show me how tall you think an umbrella is.
- What is even taller than that?
- How heavy is a cup?
- Shall we go and get one to see?

The homes that Jack built (page 40)

As a further extension activity, two sets of the cards could be used for the game, thereby introducing the possibility of 'the same height as' as well as taller and shorter. These cards could be copied, coloured and then laminated as a more permanent classroom resource. Encourage the children to talk about and observe other features of the homes, for example what shape are the windows? How many windows are there? Is the root flat or pointed? Is this home wider than this one?

SUGGESTED QUESTIONS:

- Which home is taller/shorter?
- How could we check?

At the zoo (page 41)

This sheet could be used as an assessment sheet. Notice that the word 'taller' is always used when comparing two items and 'tallest' when comparing more than two items.

SUGGESTED QUESTIONS:

- Which is taller?
- Which animal is shorter?
- Can you draw an animal that is in between?

Buckets of fun (page 42)

Use the context of this activity to explore other comparison words such as full, empty, half-full, half-empty etc. The children should work practically in the sand tray, making pairs of sandcastles and say which has more or less sand, which was made from a full or half-full bucket, or which is the larger or smaller sandcastle.

SUGGESTED QUESTIONS:

- Can you make two different-sized sandcastles?
- Which sandcastle is made using more sand?
- Was the bucket full or half-full?

A tight squeeze (page 43)

In the activity, the children could also be asked to say which car is taller or shorter each time. This will enable them to begin to realise that the concepts of taller and wider are not connected.

SUGGESTED QUESTIONS:

- Which car is wider?
- How do you know?

The three little pigs (page 44)

It is vital for comparison of how heavy things are that children have practical experience. Ensure that balance scales have been used by the children and that they appreciate that the heavier items drop lower on the balance scales than the lighter items. Have a range of different materials available so that the children begin to build up an awareness that, say, a pencil is lighter than a book, and to gain a sense of how heavy the items are.

SUGGESTED QUESTIONS:

- Which is heavier?
- How do you know?
- What can you do to check?
- Which of the two items in these scales is heavier?

The third little pig (page 45)

Encourage the children to appreciate that more or less of the same objects will mean that the total load is heavier or lighter respectively. Use sets of cubes in balance scales to ensure that the children understand this. The sheet could be used as an assessment following the practical activities.

SUGGESTED QUESTIONS:

- Which is lighter?
- How do you know?

Sunflowers (page 46)

A copy of Van Gogh's Sunflowers could be displayed on the wall and the children could paint their own sunflower pictures in art. Point out to the children that, as there are more than two sunflowers in each vase, we use the words tallest and shortest rather than taller and shorter (used for two items).

SUGGESTED QUESTIONS:

- Can you draw three flowers that are the same height?
- Which is tallest/shortest?

Sausage sizzle (page 47)

Point out to the children that, as there are more than two sausages, we use the words longest and shortest rather than longer and shorter (used for two items).

SUGGESTED QUESTION/PROMPT:

- Which is the longest/shortest sausage?
- In each question, draw a sausage that is shorter than the other three sausages.

Colourful crayons (page 48)

This sheet can be used as an assessment activity.

Watch out for children who confuse 'thinnest' with 'longest', such as in set 3 on the sheet.

SUGGESTED QUESTION/PROMPT:

- Which is the thinnest/thickest crayon?
- In each question, draw a crayon that is thicker than the other three crayons.

The longest worm (page 49)

When the children are playing this game encourage them to line up the pieces of their worm from the same end of the table to help them compare the lengths of their worms. If the children are not familiar with zero the dice could be marked 1, 2, 3, 1, 2, 3 instead, but several sheets of the worm pieces may need to be used. If such a dice is not available, use number cards.

SUGGESTED QUESTIONS:

- Who has the longest worm?
- How much longer is your worm?
- How do you know?
- How can you check?

Use everyday language related to time; order and sequence familiar events and measure short periods of time

Words that children should begin to develop an understanding of, and begin to use themselves in everyday language, include:

time, days of the week: Monday, Tuesday...
day, week, birthday, holiday, morning, afternoon,
evening, night, bedtime, dinnertime, playtime,
today, yesterday, tomorrow, before, after,
next, last, now, soon, early, late, earlier, later,
quick, quicker, quickest, quickly, first,
slow, slower, slowest, slowly,
old, older, oldest, new, newer, newest,
takes longer, takes less time, hour, o'clock,
clock, watch, hands...

Before and after pictures (page 50)

The children may be familiar with 'before' and 'after' pictures in magazines or TV programmes, such as makeovers of people or rooms in a house. This activity encourages the children to become familiar with the words 'before' and 'after' and identify which picture is which.

SUGGESTED QUESTIONS:

- Which picture is before/after?
- How do you know?

When? (page 51)

This activity is not designed to have a fixed set of correct answers. There may be more usual answers and some that are very unlikely but children should discuss their own activities and justify their answers.

SUGGESTED QUESTIONS:

- Do you usually go to the shops in the morning/afternoon/evening/night?
- Which is most likely? That you watch TV in the afternoon or in the night? That you eat lunch in the evening or in the afternoon? That you sleep in the afternoon or the night? etc.

Yesterday, today, tomorrow (page 52)

Here are some more examples you could give at the start of the lesson:

Yesterday I drew a picture.
Today I am colouring it in.
Tomorrow I will put it on the wall.
Yesterday I went to the library and chose a book.
Today I am reading it.
Tomorrow I will take it back.
Yesterday my tooth was wobbly.
Today my tooth fell out.
Tomorrow the tooth fairy will have been!
Yesterday my hair was long.
Today I am having my hair cut.
Tomorrow I will have short hair.

SUGGESTED QUESTIONS:

- What did you do yesterday?
- What are you doing today?
- What will you do tomorrow?

Which takes longer? (page 53)

This activity encourages the children to think about the length of time that things take.

SUGGESTED QUESTIONS:

- Which takes longer?
- How do you know?

In time (page 54)

This activity focuses on simple sequencing. Over the next few pages the activities contain sequences of increasing lengths. The children should glue the pictures in each sequence onto paper once ordered.

SUGGESTED QUESTIONS:

- Which picture do you think goes first?
- Why do you think that?
- Which picture is last?
- Which is in the middle?

In order (page 55)

Once the children have glued their final sequences in order ask questions about them, using words such as earlier, later, first, last, after, etc.

SUGGESTED QUESTIONS:

- Can you tell me the story shown in the pictures?
- Which picture do you think goes first?
- Why do you think that?
- Which picture is last?

Down to earth! (page 56)

This activity is more complex as it has eight pictures to sequence. Encourage the children to order several of them first and then to rearrange them as each new picture is examined.

SUGGESTED QUESTIONS:

- Can you tell me the story shown in the pictures?
- Which picture do you think goes first?
- Why do you think that?
- Which picture is last?

Just a minute (page 57)

Provide the children with experience of how long one minute is. Explore how much can be achieved in one minute, for example how many bricks can be put together, how much of a nursery rhyme can be sung, how many names of children can be said, etc. Ensure the children understand what they will be asked to do in one minute, i.e. draw two eyes on each owl. Before starting, ask them to predict how many they think they will finish. Discuss and compare their predictions. Encourage the children to compare their result with their prediction. As an extension activity, ask the children to record on plain paper how others did. Invite each child to explain how they have shown this information.

SUGGESTED QUESTIONS:

- How many owls do you think you will finish?
- How many did you finish?
- What was the highest number of owls that were finished in one minute?
- How could we show everyone's results on paper?

Good timing: 1 and 2 (pages 58 and 59)

See notes from the previous activity. In both these activities, if only a small number of shapes are drawn in a minute and there is space left on the sheet, the children could time a second minute and compare the results.

SUGGESTED QUESTIONS:

- How many squares/triangles do you think you will finish?
- How many did you finish?
- What was the highest number of shapes that were finished in one minute?

Holiday diary rhyme: 1 and 2 (pages 60 and 61)

Say this rhyme several times and invite the children to join in:

On Monday we went to the water park,
On Tuesday we went in the sea,
On Wednesday we had donkey rides,
On Thursday we watched TV,
On Friday we swam at the swimming pool,
On Saturday we played in the sun,
On Sunday we had to go home again,
But didn't we have lots of fun!

These pictures and the week-wheel can form a useful display. Some children may need help with cutting the pieces. Alternatively the pieces could be copied and laminated to keep as a more permanent classroom resource.

SUGGESTED QUESTIONS:

- What did we do on Monday?
- Which day comes after Tuesday?
- Wednesday... which comes next?

Time dominoes (pages 62)

These dominoes may only be appropriate for the more confident children who have begun to learn the order of the days of the week and are beginning to read them. Alternatively, they could be used with an adult. Encourage the children to identify which day it is today, which day it was yesterday and which day it will be tomorrow.

If copied onto thin card and laminated, the dominoes could become a more permanent classroom resource.

SUGGESTED QUESTIONS:

- Which day comes after Tuesday?
- Wednesday... which comes next?
- Can you say the days of the week in order?
- Which day is the day that comes after Saturday?

What's the time, Mr Wolf? (page 63)

As children begin to become familiar with clocks and hours and the idea of 'o'clock' this sheet could be used. Introduce the short hand, the hour hand, and explain that it shows which o'clock it is, e.g. if pointing to 4 it is 4 o'clock. The extension activity allows them opportunity to draw on the hour hand for themselves. The numbers and hands on this sheet could be masked and altered to provide more variety.

SUGGESTED QUESTIONS:

- What time does this clock show?
- Which number is the short hand, the hour hand, pointing to?
- How could you show 5 o'clock?
- Which number would the short hand be pointing to?

Homework time sheets (page 64)

This activity sheet could be taken home to be completed with the help of a parent, grandparent, carer or guardian. They should be returned and then the children's times compared. The discussion that takes place at home will help the children to appreciate how words such as hour and o'clock are used in everyday life and the importance of being able to tell the time.

SUGGESTED QUESTIONS:

- I eat breakfast at 7 o'clock.
- What time do you usually have breakfast?
- Is this before or after I do?

Using the CD-ROM

The PC CD-ROM included with this book contains an easy-to-use software program that allows you to print out pages from the book, to view them (e.g. on an interactive whiteboard) or to customise the activities to suit the needs of your pupils.

Getting started

It's easy to run the software. Simply insert the CD-ROM into your CD drive and the disk should autorun and launch the interface in your web browser.

If the disk does not autorun, open 'My Computer' and select the CD drive, then open the file 'start.html'.

Please note: this CD-ROM is designed for use on a PC. It will also run on most Apple Macintosh computers in Safari however, due to the differences between Mac and PC fonts, you may experience some unavoidable variations in the typography and page layouts of the activity sheets.

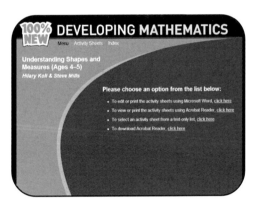

The Menu screen

Four options are available to you from the main menu screen.

The first option takes you to the Activity Sheets screen, where you can choose an activity sheet to edit or print out using Microsoft Word.

(If you do not have the Microsoft Office suite, you might like to consider using OpenOffice instead. This is a multi-platform and multi-lingual office suite, and an 'open-source' project. It is compatible with all other major office suites, and the product is free to download, use and distribute. The homepage for OpenOffice on the Internet is: www.openoffice.org.)

The second option on the main menu screen opens a PDF file of the entire book using Adobe Reader (see below). This format is ideal for printing out copies of the activity sheets or for displaying them, for example on an interactive whiteboard.

The third option allows you to choose a page to edit from a text-only list of the activity sheets, as an alternative to the graphical interface on the Activity Sheets screen.

Adobe Reader is free to download and to use. If it is not already installed on your computer, the fourth link takes you to the download page on the Adobe website.

You can also navigate directly to any of the three screens at any time by using the tabs at the top.

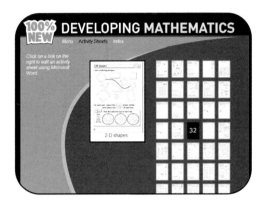

The Activity Sheets screen

This screen shows thumbnails of all the activity sheets in the book. Rolling the mouse over a thumbnail highlights the page number and also brings up a preview image of the page.

Click on the thumbnail to open a version of the page in Microsoft Word (or an equivalent software program, see above.) The full range of editing tools are available to you here to customise the page to suit the needs of your particular pupils. You can print out copies of the page or save a copy of your edited version onto your computer.

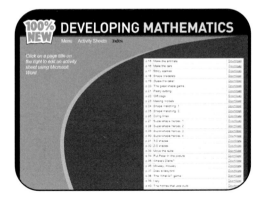

The Index screen

This is a text-only version of the Activity Sheets screen described above. Choose an activity sheet and click on the 'download' link to open a version of the page in Microsoft Word to edit or print out.

Technical support

If you have any questions regarding the *100% New Developing Literacy* or *Developing Mathematics* software, please email us at the address below. We will get back to you as quickly as possible.

educationalsales@acblack.com

Make the animals

Colour the animals.
Say what shapes have been used to make them.

NOW TRY THIS!
• **Use sticky paper shapes to make an animal of your own.**

Teachers' note Provide the children with coloured pencils. Encourage discussion of the features of the shapes such as their size, corners and using the shape names to describe them. You could ask the more confident children to colour all the triangles red, all the squares blue, etc.

100% New Developing Mathematics
Understanding Shapes and
Measures: Ages 4–5
© A & C BLACK

- ## Colour the cars.
- ## Say what shapes have been used to make them.

NOW TRY THIS!

- ## Use sticky paper shapes to make a car of your own.

Teachers' note Encourage discussion of the features of the shapes such as their size, corners and using the shape names to describe them. You could ask the more confident children to colour all the triangles red, all the squares blue, etc.

100% New Developing Mathem‹
Understanding Shapes and
Measures: Ages 4–5
© A & C BLACK

Stripy scarves

- **Colour each scarf.**
- **Use 2 or 3 colours to make a** repeating pattern **.**

NOW TRY THIS!

- **Make a repeating pattern using 4 colours.**

Teachers' note Practise saying colours in repeating patterns by starting a sequence and encouraging the children to say what comes next, for example red, blue, red, blue or red, red, blue, red, red, blue etc. You could also specify the coloured patterns you wish children to colour, for example red, yellow, red, yellow, and so on.

100% New Developing Mathematics
Understanding Shapes and
Measures: Ages 4–5
© A & C BLACK

Shape bracelets

- Colour circles red ◯ triangles blue ▷ rectangles yellow ▭
- Cut out each strip and make a bracelet.

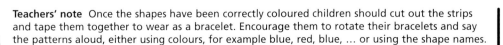

Teachers' note Once the shapes have been correctly coloured children should cut out the strips and tape them together to wear as a bracelet. Encourage them to rotate their bracelets and say the patterns aloud, either using colours, for example blue, red, blue, … or using the shape names.

100% New Developing Mathem
Understanding Shapes and
Measures: Ages 4–5
© A & C BLACK

18

Guess the cake!

Each row of cakes shows a pattern.

• Guess which cake each child will get.

• Draw the cakes to check.

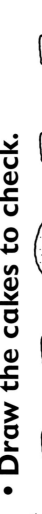

NOW TRY THIS!

• Draw another cake pattern of your own.

Teachers' note This activity encourages the children to use visual clues to continue the pattern rather than sound clues (for example circle, circle, square) as these are all cakes. If the children find this activity difficult they can be given names such as cake, donut, bun, slice… so that children can use sound clues.

100% New Developing Mathematics
Understanding Shapes and
Measures: Ages 4–5
© A & C BLACK

The great shape game

- ## Play this game with 2 friends.

☆ Cut out the pieces and share them out.

☆ Take turns to put a piece on the table.

☆ Join up the lines to make a shape.

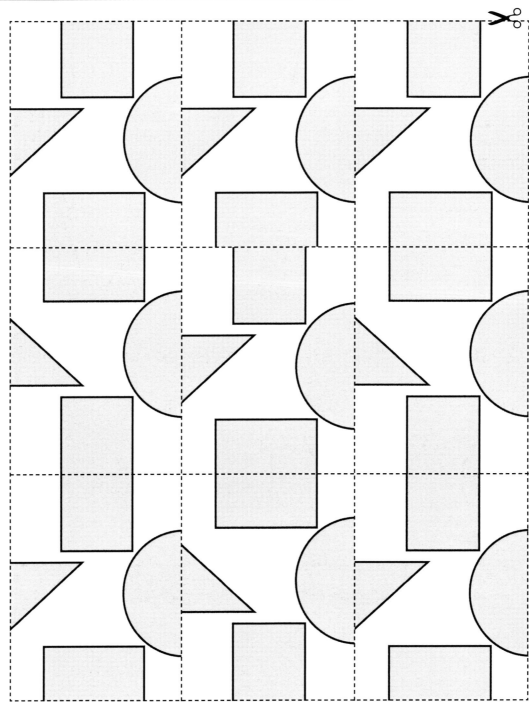

Teachers' note Encourage the children to match the sides of the shapes to make shapes that they recognise and to say the names of any shapes that they know. Note that joining two triangular pieces could make a triangle or a parallelogram. If children make the latter draw attention to the number of corners and sides it has. The game is over when all the cards have been used.

100% New Developing Mathem
Understanding Shapes and
Measures: Ages 4–5
© A & C BLACK

Pastry cutting

These shapes have been cut from pastry.

How many of each shape have been cut?

circles	triangles	rectangles	squares

3

NOW TRY THIS!

- **Draw one or more of each shape on the pastry.**

circle	triangle	rectangle	square

eachers' note This activity follows on nicely from practical pastry cutting. Pastry cutters of different shapes can be used and dough can be decorated and baked to make hard (inedible) biscuits. See page 7 for information on the simple recipe.

100% New Developing Mathematics Understanding Shapes and Measures: Ages 4–5
© A & C BLACK

Gift bags

- **These gift bags are decorated with different shapes.**

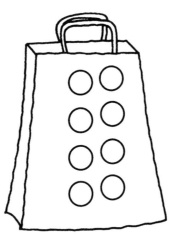
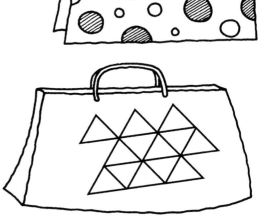

- **On these bags draw and colour some shapes. Use only one type of shape on each bag.**

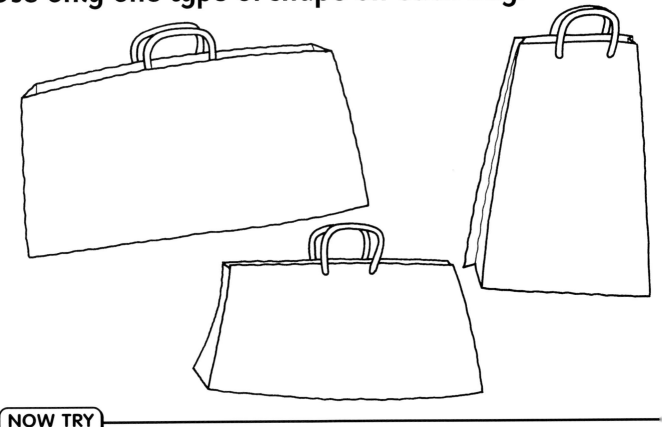

NOW TRY THIS!

- **What type of shape is on the:**
  tallest **bag?** **widest** **bag?**

Teachers' note Gift bags are a great stimulus for shape work as usually they are covered in interesting shapes or patterns. Children could make or decorate their own gift bags and should be encouraged to describe the shapes and their properties. Ask a wide range of questions using comparing words, for example 'Which bag is tallest, smallest? Which bag is thinnest, shortest?'

100% New Developing Mathem
Understanding Shapes and
Measures: Ages 4–5
© A & C BLACK

Making models

**Roll the dice and look in the box below.
Collect the matching shape.**

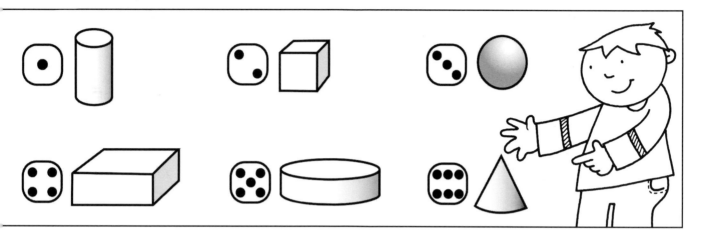

- **When you have 3 shapes, see if you can make one
  of these models with them.**
- **If not, make a model of your own.**

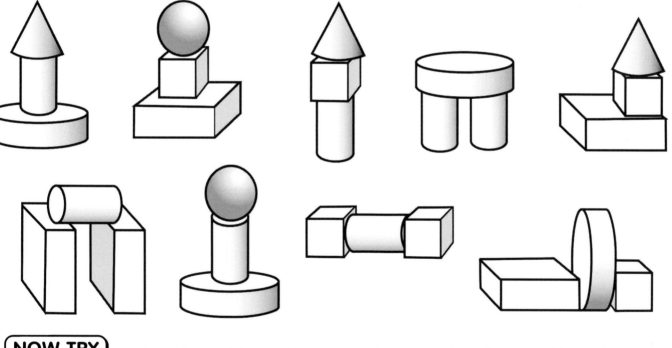

- **Roll the dice 3 more times and use all
  your shapes to make a model.**

Teachers' note Provide the children with the sets of solid shapes shown above. Encourage them
to describe the models using appropriate words such as smooth, curved, round, corners etc,
together with the shape names: cube, cuboid, sphere, cone, cylinder. This could be played as a
colouring-in game if no solid shapes are available.

**100% New Developing Mathematics
Understanding Shapes and
Measures: Ages 4–5
© A & C BLACK**

Shape matching: 1

- **Cut out the shells as carefully as you can.**
- **Match each shell with its outline on Shape matching: 2.**

Teachers' note Encourage children to describe the characteristics of the different shells using appropriate language such as smooth, round, sharp, jagged, pointy, straight, etc. and to begin to describe the shapes themselves, using words such as circle, rectangle, triangle. The sheet could be copied onto card, cut-out and laminated to be used as a more permanent resource.

100% New Developing Mathem
Understanding Shapes and
Measures: Ages 4–5
© A & C BLACK

Match the cut-out shells from Shape matching: 1 with each outline.

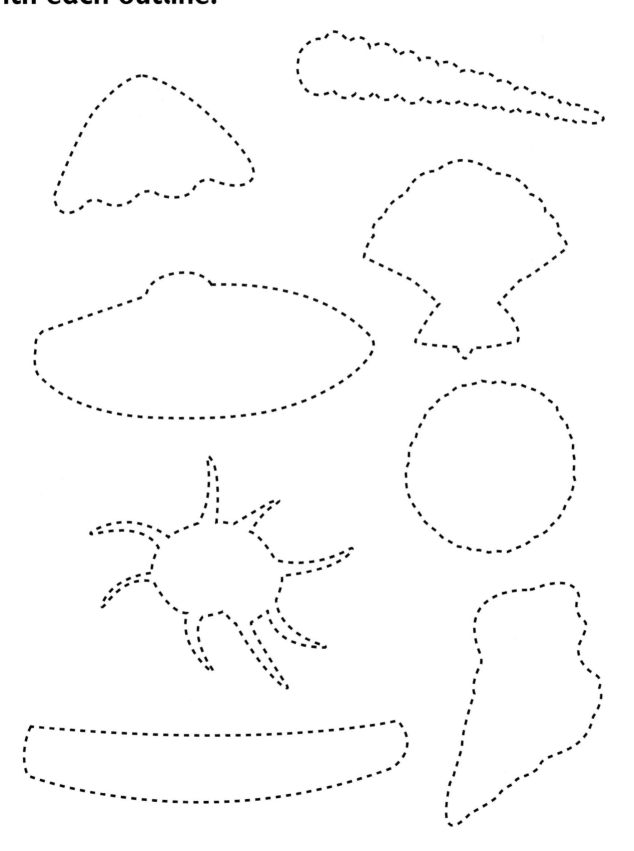

Teachers' note This sheet should be used in conjunction with page 25.

100% New Developing Mathematics
Understanding Shapes and
Measures: Ages 4–5
© A & C BLACK

25

Doing lines

- **Trace over each line.**
- **Say what is special about each line.**
- **Use some of the words in this box.** →

wavy
loopy
zigzag
curved
straight
wiggly
jagged

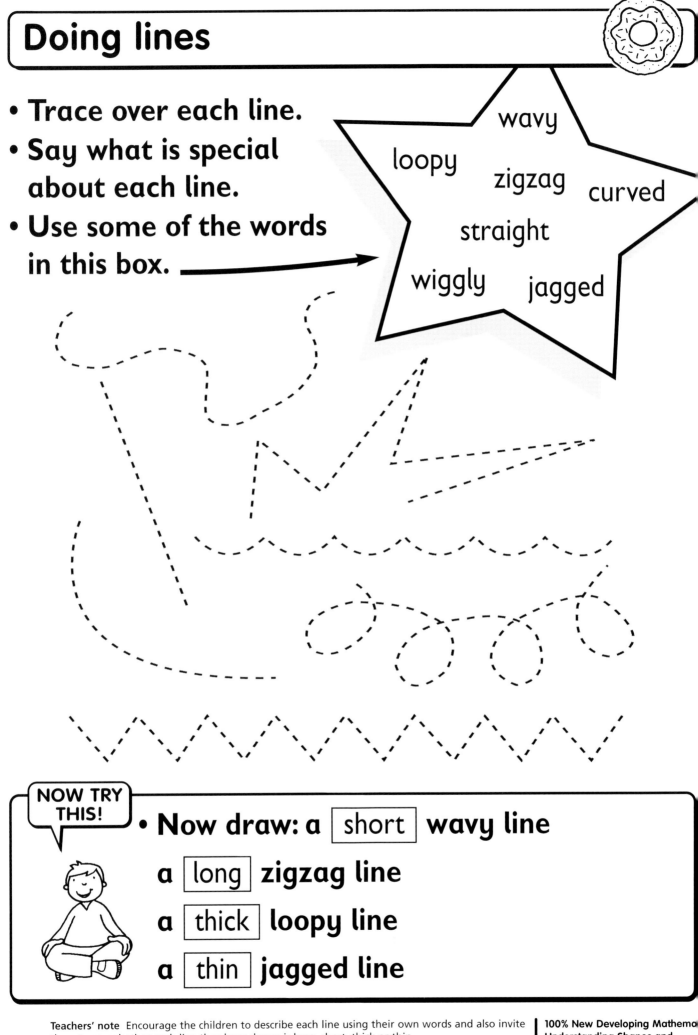

NOW TRY THIS!

- **Now draw: a** | short | **wavy line**

  a | long | **zigzag line**

  a | thick | **loopy line**

  a | thin | **jagged line**

Teachers' note Encourage the children to describe each line using their own words and also invite them to say whether each line they have drawn is long, short, thick or thin.

100% New Developing Mathema
Understanding Shapes and
Measures: Ages 4–5
© A & C BLACK

• **Colour all the parts of triangle-man's body.**
• **Count the number of triangles.**

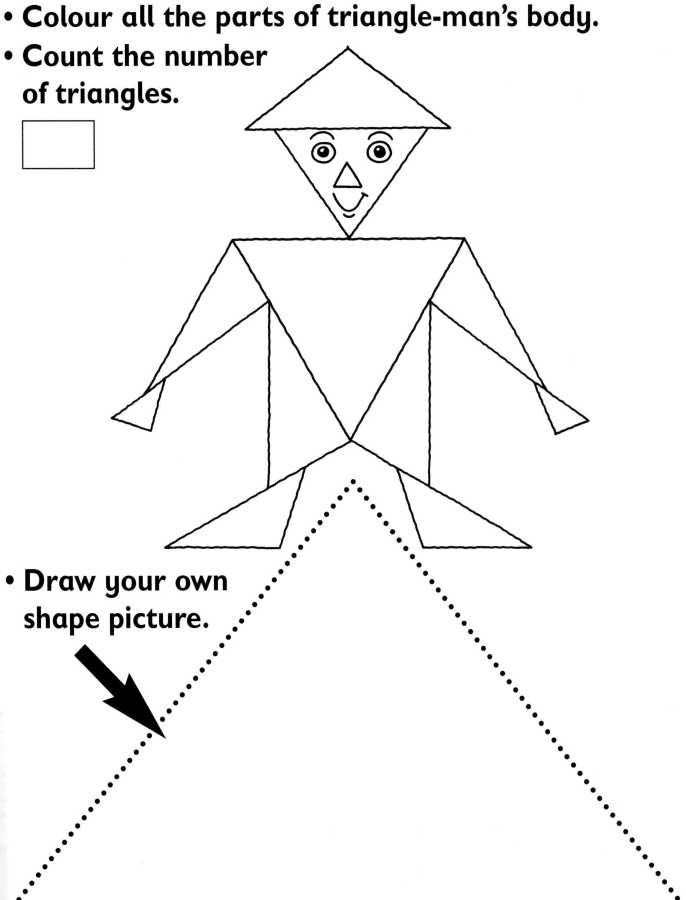

• **Draw your own shape picture.**

Teachers' note These four Super-shape heroes sheets can be used when introducing and exploring the shapes: triangles, circles, rectangles and squares. Encourage the children to describe the different sizes of the shapes, using words such as 'bigger' and 'smaller' and to draw their own shape picture inside the frame.

100% New Developing Mathematics Understanding Shapes and Measures: Ages 4–5 © A & C BLACK

- **Colour all the parts of circle-woman's body.**
- **Count the number of circles.**

- **Draw your own shape picture.**

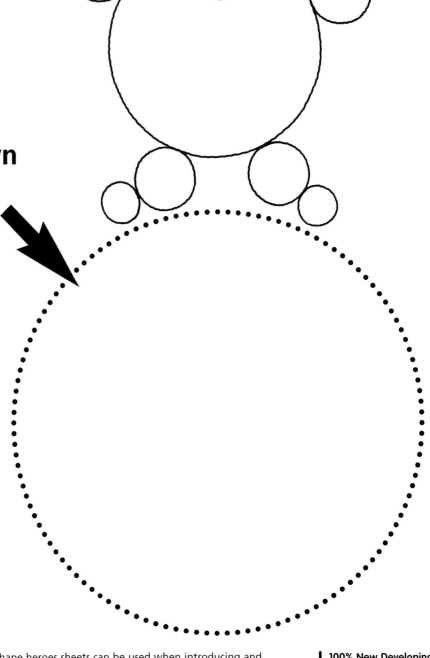

Teachers' note These four Super-shape heroes sheets can be used when introducing and exploring the shapes: triangles, circles, rectangles and squares. Encourage the children to describe the different sizes of the shapes, using words such as 'bigger' and 'smaller' and to draw their own shape picture inside the frame.

100% New Developing Mathema
Understanding Shapes and
Measures: Ages 4–5
© A & C BLACK

- **Colour all the parts of rectangle-man's body.**
- **Count the number of rectangles.**

- **Draw your own shape picture.**

Teachers' note These four Super-shape heroes sheets can be used when introducing and exploring the shapes: triangles, circles, rectangles and squares. Encourage the children to describe the different sizes of the shapes, using words such as 'bigger' and 'smaller' and to draw their own shape picture inside the frame.

100% New Developing Mathematics Understanding Shapes and Measures: Ages 4–5 © A & C BLACK

- **Colour all the parts of square-woman's body.**
- **Count the number of squares.**

- **Draw your own shape picture.**

Teachers' note These four Super-shape heroes sheets can be used when introducing and exploring the shapes: triangles, circles, rectangles and squares. Encourage the children to describe the different sizes of the shapes, using words such as 'bigger' and 'smaller' and to draw their own shape picture inside the frame.

100% New Developing Mathem
Understanding Shapes and
Measures: Ages 4–5
© A & C BLACK

3-D shapes

Join matching shapes.

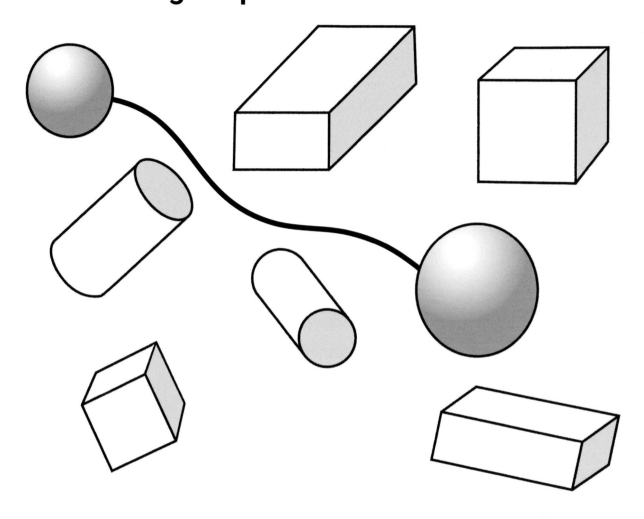

In each pair, colour the bigger shape yellow.
colour the smaller shape blue.

NOW TRY THIS!

• Tick the odd one out in each set.

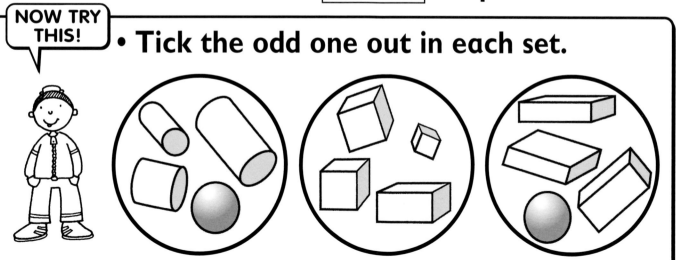

eachers' note As a further extension activity the children could use solid shapes and make their wn odd one out questions for a friend to solve. Encourage discussion of the differences between hese solid shapes and use the words cube, cuboid, cylinder, square and sphere as appropriate.

100% New Developing Mathematics
Understanding Shapes and
Measures: Ages 4–5
© A & C BLACK

2-D shapes

• **Join matching shapes.**

• **In each pair, colour the** bigger **shape yellow and colour the** smaller **shape blue.**

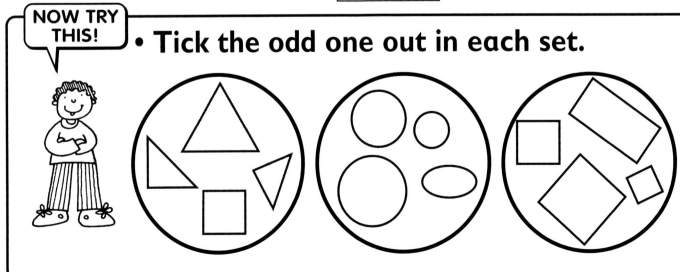

NOW TRY THIS!

• **Tick the odd one out in each set.**

Teachers' note As a further extension activity the children could draw their own odd one out questions for a friend to solve. Encourage discussion of the differences between these flat shapes and use the words circle, triangle, rectangle and square as appropriate.

100% New Developing Mathem
Understanding Shapes and
Measures: Ages 4–5
© A & C BLACK

Move the cube

on the floor	over the head	under a table
under your arm	beside a chair	next to the bin
in front of you	behind you	between your knees
in the middle of the room	near your foot	on top of a table
beneath a chair	up your sleeve	close to your nose
far from the door	above your head	opposite a door
in the bin	beneath your foot	around your head
between your hands	to the side of your head	on the bottom of your foot
on the back of your knee	above the table	at the edge of the room
in a corner of the room	under your chin	below your knees

eachers' note These cards can be used in a variety of ways to encourage use and development f the vocabulary of position and movement. See page 8 for further details.

100% New Developing Mathematics
Understanding Shapes and
Measures: Ages 4–5
© A & C BLACK

Put Peter in the picture

- **Play this game with a friend.**
- **Cut out Peter from below.**
- **Take it in turns to put Peter in the picture.**
- **Say exactly where you have put him.**

Teachers' note At the start of the lesson encourage the children to use different position words, for example beside, next to, under, over, between, on top of, near to, behind, in front of, in, on, inside, close to, at the edge of, in the middle of, far from, above, etc. Rephrase the children's sentences to show that some words mean the same thing, such as beside, next to.

100% New Developing Mathem
Understanding Shapes and
Measures: Ages 4–5
© A & C BLACK

Where's Claire?

- **Look for Claire in each picture.**
- **Say where she is.**

NOW TRY THIS!

- **Draw Claire in each of these places.**

behind a tree   under a tree   next to a tree

Teachers' note Begin by encouraging the children to use a range of different position words, for example beside, next to, under, over, between, on top of, near to, behind, in front of, in, on, inside, close to, at the edge of, in the middle of, far from, above, etc. Rephrase the children's sentences to show that similar words can mean the same thing, such as beside, next to.

100% New Developing Mathematics Understanding Shapes and Measures: Ages 4–5 © A & C BLACK

Mousey, mousey...

• **Tick the best description of where the mouse is.**

in the cup ✔

on the cup ☐

by the shoe ☐

in the shoe ☐

on the chair ☐

under the chair ☐

in the sink ☐

by the sink ☐

under the cheese ☐

next to the cheese ☐

behind the cat ☐

in front of the cat ☐

• **Draw pictures to show the mouse:**

between two cats   in front of a boy

Teachers' note Begin by discussing different position words, for example beside, next to, under, over, between, on top of, near to, behind, in front of, in, on, inside, close to, at the edge of, in the middle of, far from, above, etc. and ask the children to point to locations around the room. This activity sheet could be used as an assessment activity. Children are likely to need help with reading the words.

100% New Developing Mathem
Understanding Shapes and
Measures: Ages 4–5
© A & C BLACK

Draw a ladybird

Draw a ladybird in the places shown.

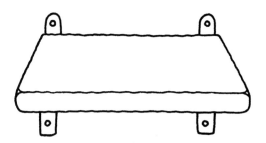

on the shelf

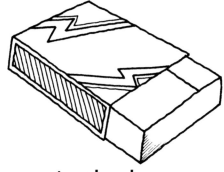

in the box

next to the butterfly

under the bench

between the flies

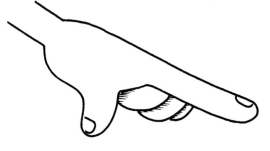

on the finger

NOW TRY THIS!

• Draw pictures to show a ladybird:

in the middle
of a leaf

opposite another
ladybird

Teachers' note Begin by discussing different position words, for example 'beside', 'next to', 'under', 'over', 'between', 'on top of', 'near to', 'behind', 'in front of', 'in', 'on', 'inside', 'close to', 'at the edge of', 'in the middle of', 'far from', 'above', etc. and ask the children to point to locations around the room. Children are likely to need help with reading the words.

100% New Developing Mathematics
Understanding Shapes and
Measures: Ages 4–5
© A & C BLACK

37

The 'What is?' game

- **Cut out the cards below.**
- **Play this game with a friend.**

What is? above	What is? below	What is? next to
What is? above	What is? below	What is? next to
What is? above	What is? below	What is? next to

Teachers' note The children play this game in pairs. They each need a set of the cards. They make a pile of 'What is?' cards and item cards. Children take turns to pick a 'What is?' card and find the object at this location in the grid. They then win this item, picking up the appropriate card. The winner is the first player to win all six items.

**100% New Developing Mathem
Understanding Shapes and
Measures: Ages 4–5
© A & C BLACK**

I spy...

• **Play this game in a small group.**

I spy something **thicker** than a book.

I spy something **smaller** than a goldfish.

Finish

 I spy something **heavier** than a cup.

I spy something **heavier** than a telephone.

I spy something **thicker** than a magazine.

I spy something **taller** than a cat.

 I spy something **lighter** than an elephant.

I spy something **longer** than my finger.

I spy something **shorter** than a door.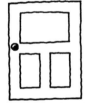

I spy something **heavier** than an apple.

I spy something **narrower** than my foot.

I spy something **wider** than my hand.

Start here I spy something **thinner** than a book.

I spy something **taller** than an umbrella.

Teachers' note Rules of the game: Players should take turns to roll the dice and move their counter forward the number of items shown on the dice. If the player can correctly point to something in the room that matches the description, they should move on one more square. If not, they should move back a square. The winner is the first to reach the finish.

100% New Developing Mathematics Understanding Shapes and Measures: Ages 4–5
© A & C BLACK

The homes that Jack built

- ## Cut out the cards.
- ## Play this game with a friend.

☆ Pick a card each.

☆ Say which building is taller and which is shorter.

☆ The player with the taller building wins both cards.

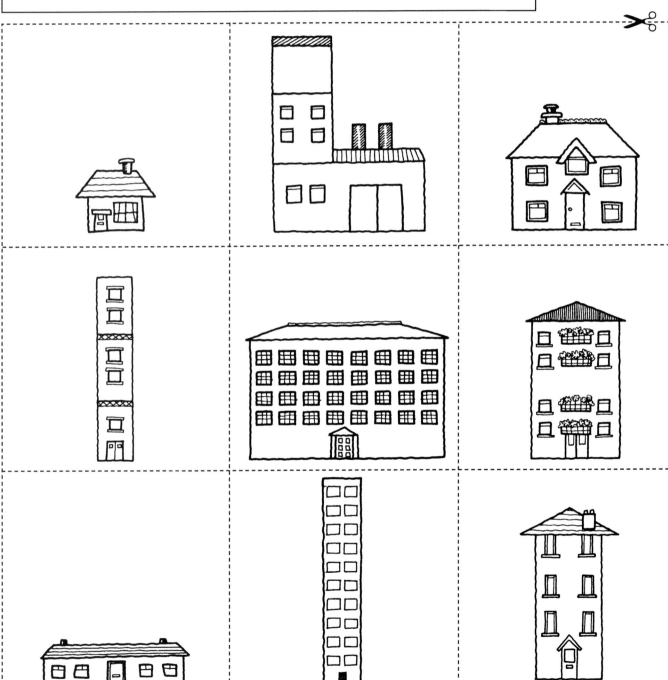

Teachers' note This activity can be linked with children's own model-making using boxes, containers and bricks to construct homes and houses of different shapes and sizes. As an extension activity, the children could put the houses in order of size. How wide or narrow each house is could also be discussed.

100% New Developing Mathem
Understanding Shapes and
Measures: Ages 4–5
© A & C BLACK

At the zoo

Colour the ⬛ taller ⬛ **animal in each pair.**

NOW TRY THIS!

• **Draw a giraffe that is** ⬛ shorter ⬛ **than this one.**

Teachers' note For the main activity, provide the children with coloured pencils. As a further extension activity, the children could draw an animal whose height is in between those animals in each pair.

100% New Developing Mathematics
Understanding Shapes and
Measures: Ages 4–5
© A & C BLACK

Buckets of fun

A bucket was used to make some sandcastles.

- **Tick which castle in each pair is made from** [more] **sand.**

- **Tick which castle in each pair is made from** [less] **sand.**

NOW TRY THIS!

- **Draw a castle that is made from** [less] **sand than this one.**

Teachers' note This activity could be used as a follow on from play activities in the sand tray. Encourage the children to make sandcastles and to say which sandcastle is made from more or less sand. The words 'full' and 'empty' can also be explored in the context of buckets.

100% New Developing Mathem
Understanding Shapes and
Measures: Ages 4–5
© A & C BLACK

42

A tight squeeze

Colour the ⬚wider⬚ car red.
Colour the ⬚narrower⬚ car blue.

- **Draw a car ⬚wider⬚ than this one.**
- **Draw a car ⬚narrower⬚ than this one.**

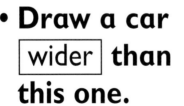

Teachers' note Discuss the terms 'wider' and 'narrower' in relation to objects around the classroom and in the environment. The word 'thinner' could also be used in place of 'narrower'.

100% New Developing Mathematics
Understanding Shapes and
Measures: Ages 4–5
© A & C BLACK

The three little pigs

- **The three little pigs are building houses of straw, wood and bricks.**
- **Tick which is heavier .**

NOW TRY THIS!

- **Draw something that is lighter than a brick.**
- **Draw something that is heavier than a brick.**

Teachers' note Ensure that children have had experience in putting things into balance scales and seeing which is heavier. This activity could follow on from the nursery rhyme The Three Little Pigs and could be used as an assessment sheet.

100% New Developing Mathema
Understanding Shapes and
Measures: Ages 4–5
© A & C BLACK

The third little pig

A pig is carrying some bricks.
Tick which load is ⬚lighter⬚ in each pair.

 **NOW TRY THIS!**
- Use cubes to make a load that is ⬚lighter⬚ than this.

eachers' note Ensure that children have practical experiences of holding and carrying wooden or lastic blocks. Discuss how the more blocks you carry the heavier the load will be, and that the wer blocks you carry the lighter the load will be.

**100% New Developing Mathematics
Understanding Shapes and
Measures: Ages 4–5**
© A & C BLACK

Sunflowers

- **Colour the** | longest | **sunflower yellow.**
- **Colour the** | shortest | **sunflower orange.**

NOW TRY THIS!

- **Draw three flowers that are the** | same length | **.**

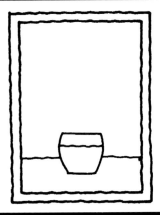

Teachers' note Encourage the children to describe the three sunflowers in each vase, saying which is the tallest, which is the shortest and describing the one in the middle using appropriate vocabulary, for example it is not the tallest, or the shortest but is in between.

46

100% New Developing Mathem
**Understanding Shapes and
Measures: Ages 4–5**
© A & C BLACK

Sausage sizzle

- **Colour the** longest **sausage brown.**
- **Colour the** shortest **sausage red.**

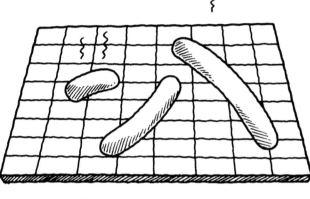

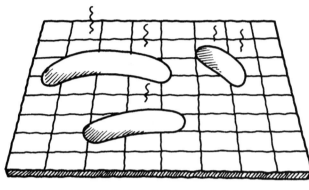

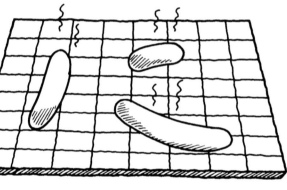

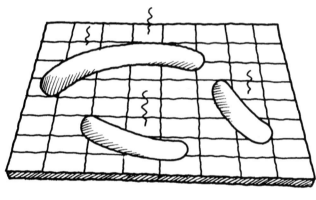

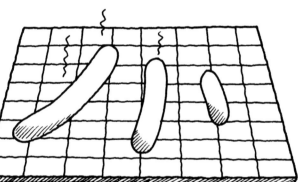

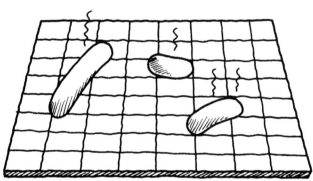

NOW TRY THIS!

- **Draw two sausages that are the** same length **.**

eachers' note Encourage the children to describe the three sausages on each barbeque, saying
hich is the longest, which is the shortest and describing the one in the middle using appropriate
ocabulary, for example it is not the longest, or the shortest but is in between.

**100% New Developing Mathematics
Understanding Shapes and
Measures: Ages 4–5**
© A & C BLACK

Colourful crayons

- **Colour the** thickest **crayon red.**
- **Colour the** thinnest **crayon yellow.**

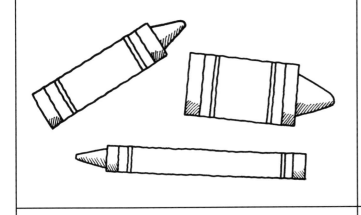
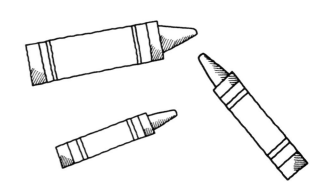

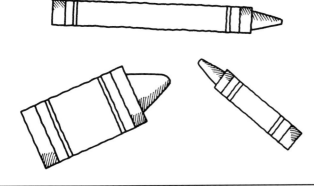
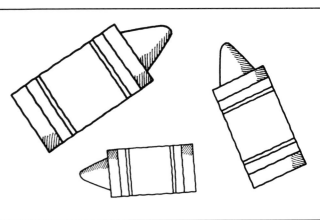

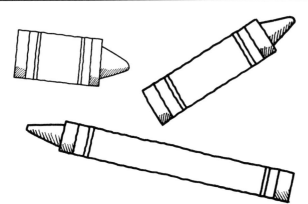

NOW TRY THIS!

- **Draw a crayon that is** thicker **than this one.**

Teachers' note Encourage the children to describe the three crayons in each set, saying which is the thickest, which is the thinnest and describing the one in the middle using appropriate vocabulary, for example it is not the thickest, or the thinnest but is in between.

48

100% New Developing Mathem
Understanding Shapes and Measures: Ages 4–5
© A & C BLACK

The longest worm

Use these cards to play
'the longest worm game'.

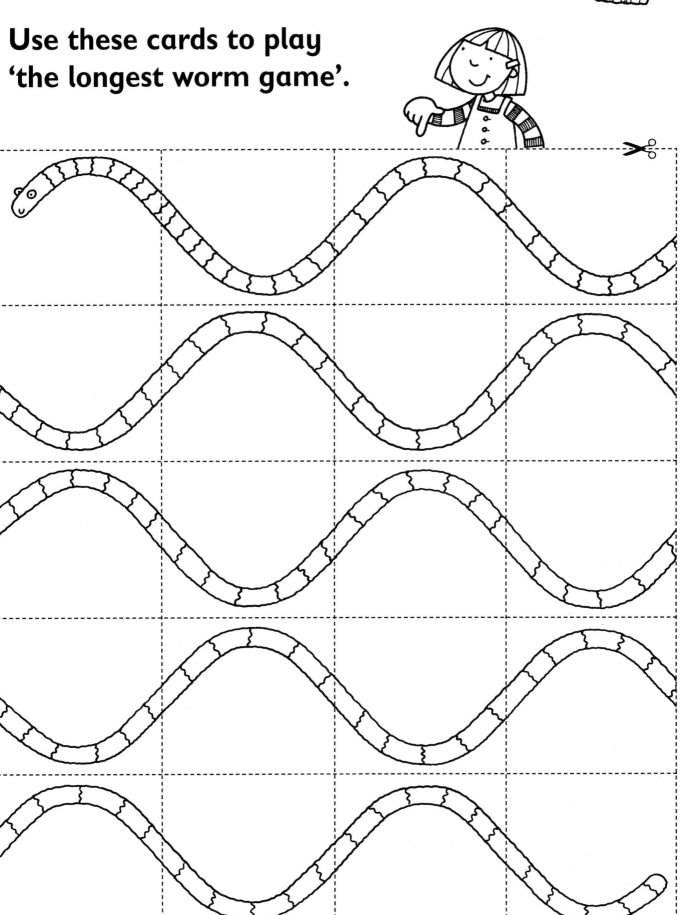

eachers' note Use the CD-Rom or copy the page to create enough pairs of worm heads and tails
or each child to have a pair. In a small group children should take turns to roll a dice, marked 0,
, 2, 0, 1, 2 and to collect that many worm pieces. At the end of each round encourage them to
iscuss whose worm is longest, shortest or in between.

**100% New Developing Mathematics
Understanding Shapes and
Measures: Ages 4–5**
© A & C BLACK

49

• **Write** <u>before</u> **and** <u>after</u> **to show which came first.**

1.

_____   _____

2.

_____   _____

3.

_____   _____

4.

_____   _____

5.

_____   _____

6.

_____   _____

NOW TRY THIS!

• **Draw two more pictures of your own.**
• **Say which is** <u>before</u> **and which is** <u>after</u>.

Teachers' note This activity can form the basis of an interesting, lively display of the children's own 'before' and 'after' pictures. 'Before' and 'after' pictures from magazines can be shown and the differences discussed. This forms the earlier part of sequencing work.

100% New Developing Mathem
Understanding Shapes and
Measures: Ages 4–5
© A & C BLACK

When?

- **Look at each picture.**
- **Say at which times of day you usually do that activity.**
- **Use these words.**

| morning | afternoon | evening | night |

eat breakfast

sleep

have a bath

leave school

clean your teeth

get up

go to school

watch TV

go to bed

go to the shops

play on the computer

eat lunch

Teachers' note Ask questions about each picture to encourage the children to think about each event: 'Would you have breakfast in the evening?' 'Would you go to school at night?' etc. It is important that the children realise that some of these activities could be done at different times of the day, for example you clean your teeth in the morning and in the evening.

100% New Developing Mathematics Understanding Shapes and Measures: Ages 4–5 © A & C BLACK

Yesterday, today, tomorrow

• **Match each sentence with a picture.**

Yesterday **I bought some wood.**

Today **I am building a toy box.**

Tomorrow **I will put toys in it.**

NOW TRY THIS!

• **Write your own sentences.**
• **Draw some pictures.**

Yesterday I _____

Today I am _____

Tomorrow I will _____

Teachers' note Ensure that children have had plenty of experience in using these words. At the start of the lesson introduce several of these sentences, for example 'Yesterday I bought a bike.' 'Today I fell off the bike.' 'Tomorrow I will have a bruise on my knee.' **or** 'Yesterday we drove to the seaside.' 'Today we are swimming in the sea.' 'Tomorrow we will go home again'.

100% New Developing Mathem
Understanding Shapes and
Measures: Ages 4–5
© A & C BLACK

Which takes longer?

Tick ✔ which takes longer .

washing
your hands

or

eating
your lunch

☐ ☐

2.

 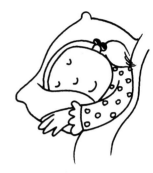

brushing
your teeth

or

sleeping

☐ ☐

going
shopping

or

brushing
your hair

☐ ☐

4.

going
swimming

or

putting on
your shoes

☐ ☐

NOW TRY THIS!

• **Draw something
that takes longer
to do than writing
your name.**

Teachers' note Children need to begin to appreciate the length of periods of time and begin to recognise which events take longer than others. Ensure that the lengths of time of classroom activities are discussed, for example 'Does it take a long time or a short time for me to do the register?' 'Does it take longer to eat your lunch?' etc.

**100% New Developing Mathematics
Understanding Shapes and
Measures: Ages 4–5
© A & C BLACK**

In time

- **Cut out the pictures in each strip.**
- **Put them in order starting with the picture that comes first.**

Teachers' note Encourage the children to draw their own sequence pictures to show the order in which things might happen. Use vocabulary such as 'before', 'after', 'earlier', 'later', 'next', 'yesterday', 'today', 'tomorrow' to discuss events. Talk about how some sequences could occur in both directions such as the foot sequence, and others could not, for example the plant sequence.

54

100% New Developing Mathem
**Understanding Shapes and
Measures: Ages 4–5**
© A & C BLACK

In order

Cut out the cards and put the two stories in order.

Teachers' note Note that the cards on this page form two different sequences. The cards could be coloured and then laminated to be used as a more permanent classroom resource.

**100% New Developing Mathematics
Understanding Shapes and
Measures: Ages 4–5
© A & C BLACK**

Down to earth!

- ## Cut out the cards and put them in order.

Teachers' note The children should work with a partner to sequence these cards. Encourage them to use words such as 'before' and 'after' and to say what event came first or last. The cards could be coloured and then laminated to be used as a more permanent classroom resource.

100% New Developing Mathem
Understanding Shapes and
Measures: Ages 4–5
© A & C BLACK

Just a minute

Use a **1-minute** sand timer.
Carefully draw 2 eyes on each owl.

NOW TRY THIS!

- **Count how many owls you finished.** ☐
- **How many eyes did you draw?** ☐

---

achers' note First show the children how to use a one-minute sand timer or alternatively you
uld say 'start' and 'stop' after 1 minute.

100% New Developing Mathematics
Understanding Shapes and
Measures: Ages 4–5
© A & C BLACK

Good timing: 1

- Use a **1**-minute sand timer.
- Carefully draw as many
  | squares | as you can below.

NOW TRY
THIS!

- **Count how many squares you finished.** ☐

Teachers' note This activity encourages the children to develop a sense of the length of time of a minute and to begin to appreciate what can be achieved in that time. Discuss how the sizes of the squares they choose to draw can vary, but they should try to draw as many squares as possible.

100% New Developing Mathem
Understanding Shapes and
Measures: Ages 4–5
© A & C BLACK

Good timing: 2

Use a 1-minute sand timer.
Carefully draw as many
| triangles | as you can below.

NOW TRY THIS!

- **Count how many triangles you finished.**

eachers' note At the start of the lesson, ask the children to explain what a triangle is. This
ctivity encourages the children to develop a sense of the length of time of a minute and to
egin to appreciate what can be achieved in that time. Discuss how the sizes of the triangles they
hoose to draw can vary, but they should try to draw as many triangles as possible.

100% New Developing Mathematics
Understanding Shapes and
Measures: Ages 4–5
© A & C BLACK

Holiday diary rhyme: 1

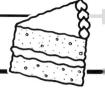

On ⬚ Monday ⬚ we went to the water park,

On ⬚ Tuesday ⬚ we went in the sea,

On ⬚ Wednesday ⬚ we had donkey rides,

On ⬚ Thursday ⬚ we watched TV,

On ⬚ Friday ⬚ we swam at the swimming pool,

On ⬚ Saturday ⬚ we played in the sun,

On ⬚ Sunday ⬚ we had to go home again,

But didn't we have lots of fun!

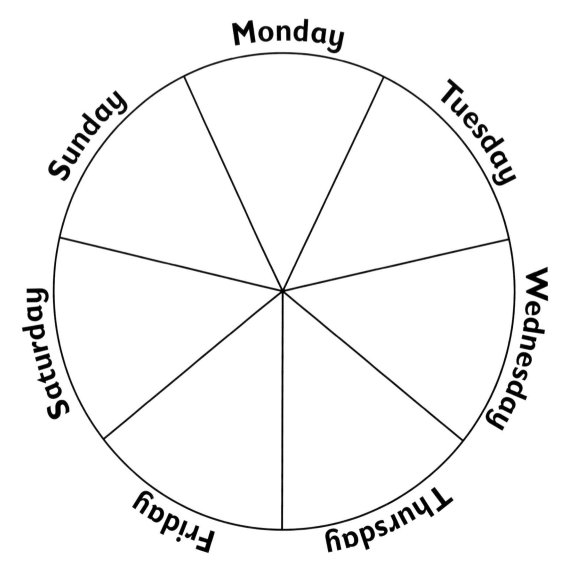

Teachers' note Say this rhyme many times so that the children become familiar with it. Each time you say it encourage the children to shout the name of the days of the week. Provide each child with a copy of this and the following sheet and ask them to match up the pictures with each day of the week according to the rhyme. Repeat the rhyme many times as they are cutting and sticking.

100% New Developing Mathem **Understanding Shapes and** **Measures: Ages 4–5** © A & C BLACK

Cut out the pictures.
Stick them in the wheel to match the rhyme.

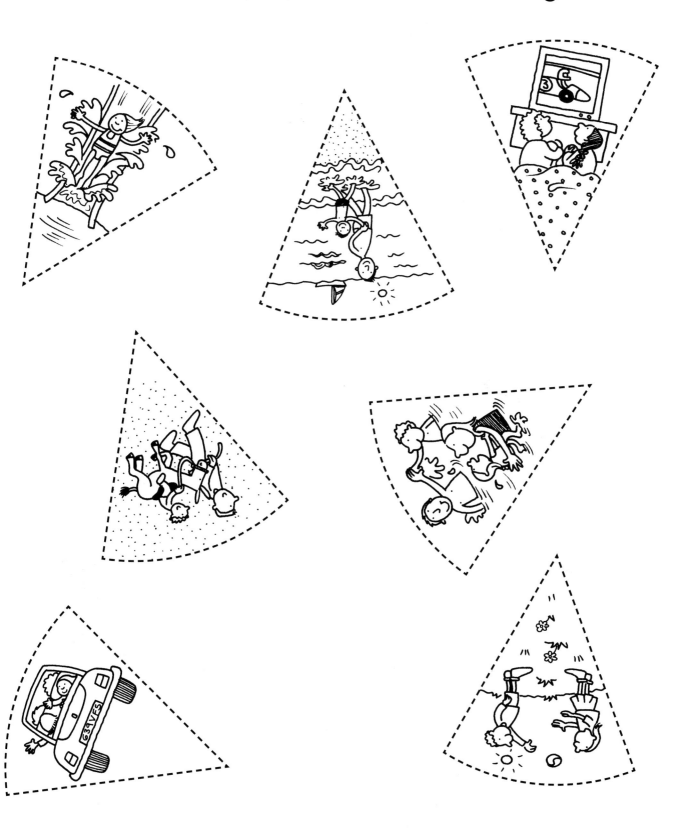

achers' note This sheet should be used in conjunction with page 60.

**100% New Developing Mathematics
Understanding Shapes and
Measures: Ages 4–5**
© A & C BLACK

Time dominoes

- ## Cut out the dominoes.
- ## Play this game with a friend.

Thursday	The day after Thursday is… 
Wednesday	The day after Wednesday is… 
Tuesday	The day after Tuesday is… 
Saturday	The day after Saturday is… 
Sunday	The day after Sunday is… 
Monday	The day after Monday is… 
Friday	The day after Friday is… 

Teachers' note Ask the children to find the domino showing Monday and to put it in the middle of the table. Share out the other dominoes. Tell the children to take turns to try and lay the next domino and put them all in order. This worksheet could be used as a follow-on activity to page 60. It could also be given as a homework activity.

100% New Developing Mathe **Understanding Shapes and** **Measures: Ages 4–5** © A & C BLACK

What's the time, Mr Wolf?

Mr Wolf is telling the time.
Help him by filling in the numbers.

☐ o'clock

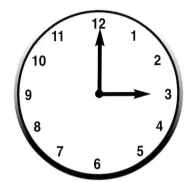

☐ o'clock

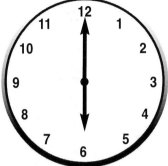

☐ o'clock

☐ o'clock

☐ o'clock

☐ o'clock

NOW TRY THIS!

• **Draw the short hand (hour hand) to show these times.**

2 o'clock

9 o'clock

11 o'clock

achers' note This activity may only be suitable for those children who have already begun to
ppreciate how the hands of a clock display time. It is important that children are familiar with
e words o'clock and hour (short) hand before tackling this kind of activity.

100% New Developing Mathematics
Understanding Shapes and
Measures: Ages 4–5
© A & C BLACK

Homework time sheets

- **Please can you help me fill in these clocks to the nearest hour, to show what time I do these things on a normal school day.**
- **My teacher says 'Thank you.'**

I wake up at

I have breakfast at

I go to school a

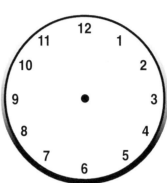

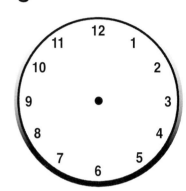

I come home at

I eat dinner at

I go to bed at

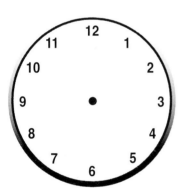

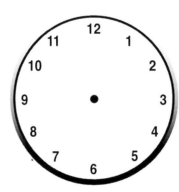

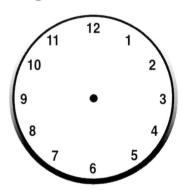

NOW TRY THIS!

- **This is a picture of me at ⬚ o'clock.**

Teachers' note For the activity at the bottom, ask the children to draw a picture of what they usually do at a certain time. This could be one of the activities shown above or other things, such as watching TV or listening to a story etc.

100% New Developing Mathe
**Understanding Shapes and
Measures: Ages 4–5**
© A & C BLACK